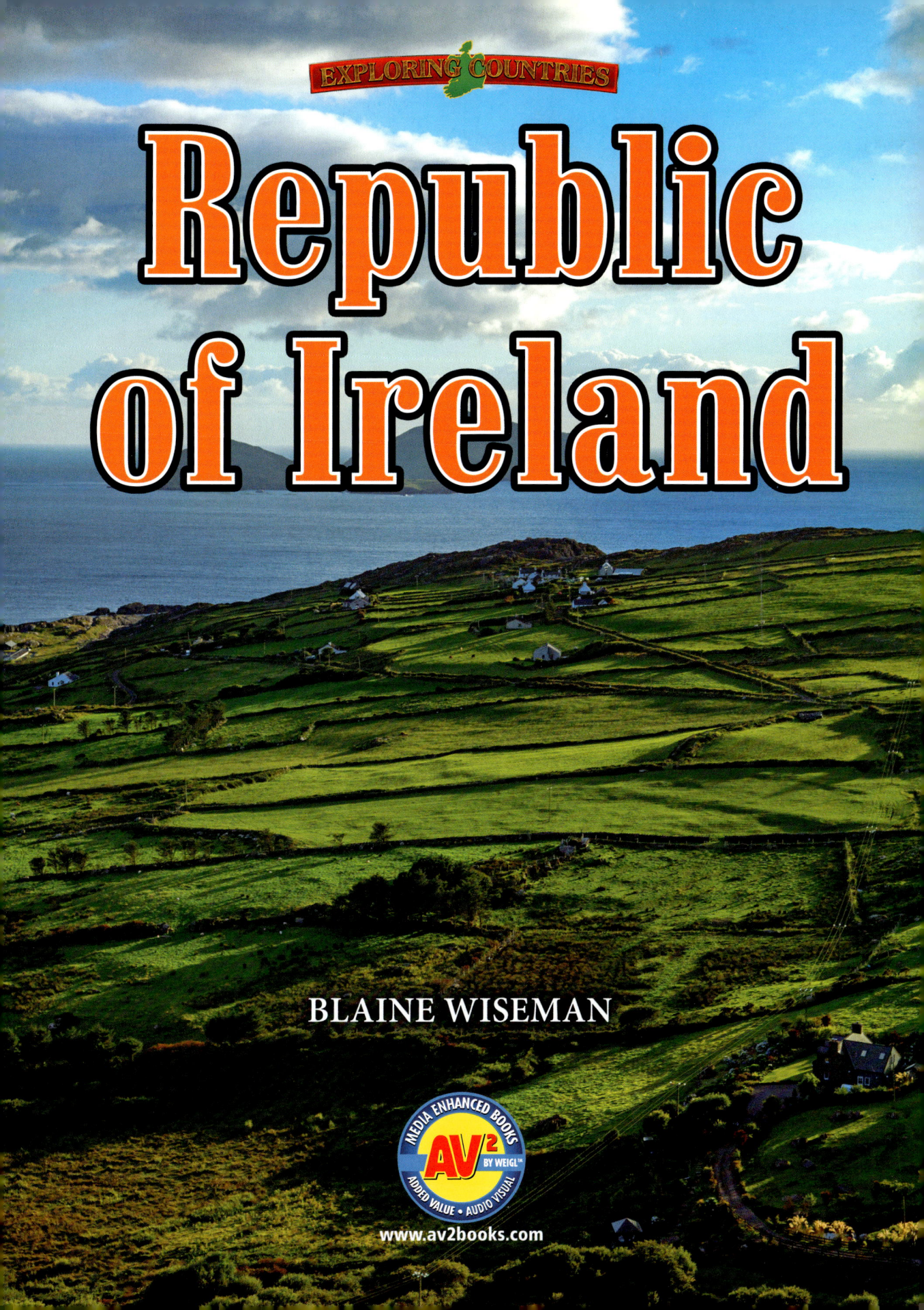

AV² provides enriched content that supplements and complements this book. Weigl's AV² books strive to create inspired learning and engage young minds in a total learning experience.

Your AV² Media Enhanced books come alive with...

Audio
Listen to sections of the book read aloud.

Key Words
Study vocabulary, and complete a matching word activity.

Video
Watch informative video clips.

Quizzes
Test your knowledge.

Embedded Weblinks
Gain additional information for research.

Slideshow
View images and captions, and prepare a presentation.

Try This!
Complete activities and hands-on experiments.

... and much, much more!

Go to www.av2books.com, and enter this book's unique code.

BOOK CODE

AVL49645

AV² by Weigl brings you media enhanced books that support active learning.

Published by AV² by Weigl
350 5th Avenue, 59th Floor
New York, NY 10118
Website: www.av2books.com

Copyright © 2020 AV² by Weigl
All rights reserved. No part of this publication may be reproduced, stored in a retrieval system, or transmitted in any form or by any means, electronic, mechanical, photocopying, recording, or otherwise, without the prior written permission of the publisher.

Library of Congress Control Number: 2019938457

ISBN 978-1-7911-0906-6 (hardcover)
ISBN 978-1-7911-0907-3 (softcover)
ISBN 978-1-7911-0908-0 (multi-user eBook)
ISBN 978-1-7911-0909-7 (single-user eBook)

Printed in Guangzhou, China
1 2 3 4 5 6 7 8 9 0 23 22 21 20 19

062019
311018

Editor Heather Kissock
Art Director Terry Paulhus
Layout Tammy West

Photo Credits
Every reasonable effort has been made to trace ownership and to obtain permission to reprint copyright material. The publishers would be pleased to have any errors or omissions brought to their attention so that they may be corrected in subsequent printings.

Weigl acknowledges Getty Images, Alamy, Newscom, and Shutterstock as its primary photo suppliers for this title.

Contents

AV² Book Code 2	Road to Independence 18
Republic of Ireland Overview 4	Population 20
Exploring the Republic of Ireland 6	Politics and Government 21
	Cultural Groups 22
Land and Climate 8	Arts and Entertainment 24
Plants and Animals 10	Sports 26
Natural Resources 11	Mapping the Republic of Ireland 28
Tourism 12	
Industry 14	Quiz Time 30
Goods and Services 15	Key Words 31
Indigenous Peoples 16	Index 31
Viking Invasion 17	Log on to www.av2books.com 32

Republic of Ireland Overview

The **Republic** of Ireland is found on the southern end of Ireland, one of the many islands that comprise the British Isles. The country is usually referred to, simply, as Ireland. Made up of rolling green hills, jagged coastlines, and hundreds of smaller islands, Ireland is known for its culture as much as its geography. Irish music, literature, and dance have provided the country with a unique character that is world-renowned. While the Irish people embrace their traditions, they keep a **progressive** outlook. As a result, Ireland has one of the fastest-growing **economies** in the **European Union** (EU) and ranks as one of the wealthiest countries in the world.

People from all over the world come to Dublin to shop on Grafton Street. Centrally located, it offers a variety of shops, ranging from department stores to small boutiques.

Muckross House, located in the Killarney area, is one of many Irish manor houses open to the public.

Irish stew is traditionally made with mutton and served with Irish soda bread.

Jaunting cars were created in Ireland in the late 18th century. Today, they are used mainly for the country's tourist trade.

Irish music is passed down from generation to generation. It is not uncommon for people to get together for a jam session.

Republic of Ireland 5

Exploring the Republic of Ireland

The Republic of Ireland covers a total area of 27,132 square miles (70,272 square kilometers). It is the 23rd-largest country in the EU. Ireland shares the island with Northern Ireland, a country in the United Kingdom. The republic accounts for about 80 percent of the island. It is divided into 26 counties. Northern Ireland is the country's only land border. The rest of Ireland is surrounded by water. The Atlantic Ocean lies to the west and north, the Irish Sea to the east, and the Celtic Sea to the south.

Achill Island

River Shannon

Carrauntoohil

Map Legend
- Republic of Ireland
- Capital City
- Land
- Carrauntoohil
- Water
- River Shannon

SCALE
250 Miles
250 Kilometers

Achill Island

Covering an area of 56 square miles (145 sq. km), Achill Island is Ireland's largest island. Located just off Ireland's west coast, the island is connected to the mainland by the Michael Davitt Bridge.

River Shannon

At a length of 161 miles (259 km), the Shannon is Ireland's longest river. Its source is the pools at the base of Tiltinbane Mountain, in County Cavan. From there, it winds south before draining into the Atlantic Ocean.

Carrauntoohil

Rising 3,406 feet (1,038 meters), Carrauntoohil is Ireland's tallest mountain. It is found within the MacGillycuddy's Reeks mountain range in County Kerry. A 16-foot (5-m) tall cross stands on top of Carrauntoohil, greeting hikers who reach the summit.

Dublin

Located at the mouth of the River Liffey, Dublin was first settled more than 1,000 years ago. Today, the city serves as the country's capital, as well as its financial and cultural center.

Republic of Ireland 7

PLANTS AND ANIMALS

While Ireland's grasses receive most of the attention, the country is home to a wide variety of plant life. Butterwort, bell heather, and sundew are common in the boglands. The highlands are home to sturdy plants such as saxifrage and sheep's bit. Forests of oak once blanketed the country, but most were cleared over time and used for shipbuilding and fuel. In recent years, the government has begun a replanting program. Most of the new trees are Sitka spruce.

One of the larger land **mammals** native to Ireland is the red deer. Other native mammals include the red fox and the Irish hare. Rodents such as shrews, mice, and squirrels are found throughout the land. These small mammals provide food for peregrine falcons, sparrowhawks, barn owls, and other birds of prey.

The waters of Ireland are home to a wide variety of aquatic life. Dolphins, whales, and sharks can often be seen in the bays and ocean waters off the coast. Salmon and trout swim up Ireland's rivers to **spawn**. Other fish **species** native to Ireland include pike and perch.

Plants and Animals by the Numbers

0 Number of snakes native to Ireland.

11% Portion of the republic now covered in forests.

3 Leaves on a shamrock, the Republic of Ireland's national symbol.

Four types of deer live in Ireland. Of these four, only the red deer is considered a native species.

Exploring Countries

NATURAL RESOURCES

The Republic of Ireland's main natural resources are **minerals** and energy sources. Ireland is one of the largest zinc-producing countries in Europe and is home to the continent's biggest zinc mine. Zinc is sold all over the world to manufacturers of cars and construction equipment, and to many other industries that require strong, flexible metal. Other minerals found in Ireland include lead, silver, and gypsum.

Ireland has abundant energy resources as well. Peat has been an important fuel source in Ireland for centuries. While most Irish homes today are powered and heated with electricity, Ireland is still the second-largest consumer of peat in the world. The country also has vast stores of natural gas. About half of all the electricity used in Ireland is supplied by this resource. With the push toward using **renewable energy**, the republic has invested in the development of wind farms. They now generate about 24 percent of the country's electricity.

349.9 billion Estimated amount of natural gas Ireland has in cubic feet. (9.91 billion cubic meters)

1992 Year Ireland built its first wind farm, at Bellacorick.

30,000 Number of people employed in Ireland's natural resources sector.

Once it is dug up, peat is stacked and left to dry. This can take several months. However, the peat will not burn well if it is not completely dry.

TOURISM

Ireland attracts tourists from all over the world. They visit the country to experience its vibrant culture and history, and to enjoy the many sights and attractions. From the cobblestone streets of Dublin to the grass-covered sandstone cliffs of the highlands, Ireland offers visitors a wide variety of experiences.

The most popular destination for tourists is Dublin, Ireland's largest city. As modern as Dublin is, the city retains strong connections to its past, with many of its historic landmarks still in use today. Dublin Castle has been an important government facility in Ireland since the 13th century. Founded in 1592, Trinity College remains Ireland's most prestigious university. St. Stephen's Green is Ireland's best-known city park, and has been since 1880.

Ireland's second-largest city, Cork, is another popular place to visit. This city on the southeastern coast often refers to itself as the "real capital of Ireland." An important seaport, Cork is a city of hillside markets and churches, and beautiful ocean views. Nearby is Blarney Castle, where tourists line up to kiss its famous Blarney Stone.

Trinity College is home to the ancient *Book of Kells*. It is believed that the religious book was written in about 800 AD.

Legend says that anyone who kisses the Blarney Stone will receive the gift of eloquence. Every year, up to 400,000 people line up to receive their gift.

Across the island on the southwest coast lies the Dingle **Peninsula**. Here, tourists can walk along sandy beaches, look out over the water, and watch dolphins play in the bay. People can also visit the area's villages, where traditional Irish life is still alive and well.

The northwest city of Galway also attracts many visitors. While the city itself has plenty to offer tourists, its main attraction is the nearby Cliffs of Moher. Bus tours take visitors through the region known as the Burren, where they can see lighthouses, castles, and caves, before peering over the edge of the cliffs.

While tourism is a major industry year-round in Ireland, it reaches its peak every March 17. Millions of visitors flock to Dublin, Cork, Galway, and other Irish cities and towns to celebrate St. Patrick's Day. Parades, live music, fireworks, and parties help the Irish and everyone else toast the country's patron saint.

Tourism by the Numbers

11.2 million
Number of overseas visitors who came to Ireland in 2018.

1204 Year Dublin Castle was founded.

323,000 Approximate number of people who passed through Dublin's airport in the days surrounding St. Patrick's Day 2018.

The Burren is also the site of the Poulnabrone Dolmen. Built approximately 5,800 years ago, the structure was once part of a tomb. The remains of 21 people have been found at the site.

Republic of Ireland 13

INDUSTRY

For a long time, agriculture drove Ireland's economy. Today, it continues to play an important role in generating income for the country. Most of Ireland's farms are family-owned and operated. A small portion are owned by large corporations. Cattle are the main **commodity** in this sector, with both beef and dairy cows making up large parts of the industry. Wheat, barley, beets, potatoes, pigs, chickens, and sheep are some of the other major resources grown and tended by Irish farmers.

In recent years, Ireland's technology sector has grown into one of Europe's largest. Many of the world's most powerful technology companies, including Google and Facebook, have their European head offices in Dublin. Much of the industry is centered in an area of Dublin known as the Silicon Docks. Here, technological giants work alongside small **start-up** companies.

Industry by the Numbers

139,600 Approximate number of farms in Ireland.

8.6% Percentage of Ireland's workers employed in agriculture.

MORE THAN 700 Number of U.S. companies with offices in Ireland.

In 2018, Facebook announced its plans to expand its Irish operations, adding another 5,000 employees to the more than 4,000 people already working there.

GOODS AND SERVICES

In 2018 alone, Ireland **exported** $165 billion worth of goods to other countries. More than 50 percent of these goods were shipped to other European countries. North American countries accounted for about 30 percent. Irish goods were also exported to countries in Asia, Oceania, and Latin America. Key Irish exports include machinery and medical equipment.

Ireland also **imports** products from other countries. Even though the country has its own stores of natural gas, it still imports fuel from other countries. The bulk of these imports is in the form of fossil fuels, such as processed petroleum and crude oil. Vehicles and electrical equipment are also imported.

At the end of 2018, Ireland's **employment rate** stood at almost 70 percent. Most people were employed in the country's service sector. People in this sector provide services to others. Jobs in the service sector range from truck drivers to bankers to chefs.

Goods and Services by the Numbers

1.5 million Number of Irish workers employed in the service sector.

#1 Ireland's ranking on the list of fastest-growing economies in the **eurozone**.

$48.8 Billion Total value of Irish exports to the United States in 2018.

Dublin has the country's largest seaport. Almost two-thirds of Ireland's port traffic travels through it.

Cultural Groups

Despite centuries of English control, Ireland has been able to maintain its own unique identity and culture. The country has two official languages, Irish and English. Irish, however, is considered the nation's first official language. This designation pays tribute to Ireland's Celtic past. Irish comes from the Gaelic language that was spoken by the Celts. Only about five percent of Irish people speak the Irish language on a regular basis, but it can be seen and heard throughout the country. English is Ireland's most widely spoken language.

Some parts of Ireland have a mix of unilingual and bilingual road signs.

Ireland has a strong base of people who want to ensure the Irish language survives into the future. Demonstrations are sometimes staged to encourage more government funding in this area.

Exploring Countries

The most common place for visitors to see the Irish language in practice is on road signs. Any traffic sign in Ireland with words must include Irish. Most signs have the Irish language in italics with the English in large letters underneath. However, there are some parts of Ireland that have Irish-only road signs. These areas are called Gaeltachtai.

Scattered throughout Ireland, Gaeltachtai are where large numbers of people still speak Irish as their main language. The most populous Gaeltacht is around Galway, on the country's west coast. Other major Gaeltachtai can be found in the counties of Cork, Clare, and Mayo. These areas are officially recognized and protected by the Irish government.

Ireland is also home to many other cultural groups. Polish people make up the largest minority group in Ireland. There are also small pockets of people from Romania, Lithuania, Latvia, Brazil, and the United Kingdom. Most immigrants live in or near Dublin, helping it to become one of Europe's most **cosmopolitan** and **multicultural** cities. Up to 200 languages are spoken in the city.

Cultural Groups BY THE NUMBERS

122,515 Number of Polish people living in Ireland, making up more than 2.5 percent of the population.

40% Portion of Irish people who speak Irish.

612,018 Number of people in Ireland who speak a language other than Irish or English at home.

The Polish community has established a presence in Dublin, with many immigrants starting businesses of their own.

SPORTS

The Irish people watch and participate in a variety of sports. None of these sports, however, bring out Irish passion like the ones invented in Ireland. The Gaelic Athletic Association (GAA) was founded in 1884 to promote traditional Irish sports. Since its founding, Gaelic football and hurling have grown to become two of the most popular sports in the country.

Gaelic football has been played in Ireland for hundreds of years. There are various forms of the game, but all of them combine elements of soccer and rugby. The game is played on a rectangular grass pitch, or field, with two teams of 15 each vying for control of a round football. Points are scored when a team passes the ball through or over the other team's goal post.

Dublin midfielder Brian Howard is one of the GAA's top football players. He was named an All-Star in his first season as a starter.

Known as the fastest game on grass, hurling is a mix of lacrosse, baseball, and field hockey. Like Gaelic football, the game is played by two teams of 15 players. A team scores points by getting a baseball-sized ball across the other team's goal post. While Gaelic football players use their hands and feet to do this, hurling players use a stick that curves at one end. This stick is called a hurley.

The 2018 GAA All-Ireland Senior Hurling Championship Final featured teams from Galway and Limerick. The match ended with Limerick winning its eighth title, its first since 1973.

26 Exploring Countries

SPORTS

The Irish people watch and participate in a variety of sports. None of these sports, however, bring out Irish passion like the ones invented in Ireland. The Gaelic Athletic Association (GAA) was founded in 1884 to promote traditional Irish sports. Since its founding, Gaelic football and hurling have grown to become two of the most popular sports in the country.

Gaelic football has been played in Ireland for hundreds of years. There are various forms of the game, but all of them combine elements of soccer and rugby. The game is played on a rectangular grass pitch, or field, with two teams of 15 each vying for control of a round football. Points are scored when a team passes the ball through or over the other team's goal post.

Dublin midfielder Brian Howard is one of the GAA's top football players. He was named an All-Star in his first season as a starter.

Known as the fastest game on grass, hurling is a mix of lacrosse, baseball, and field hockey. Like Gaelic football, the game is played by two teams of 15 players. A team scores points by getting a baseball-sized ball across the other team's goal post. While Gaelic football players use their hands and feet to do this, hurling players use a stick that curves at one end. This stick is called a hurley.

The 2018 GAA All-Ireland Senior Hurling Championship Final featured teams from Galway and Limerick. The match ended with Limerick winning its eighth title, its first since 1973.

26 Exploring Countries

Irish music has helped to spread Irish culture all over the world. Bands such as The Dubliners and The Chieftains found success playing traditional Irish folk songs, often featuring instruments such as uilleann pipes, fiddles, tin whistles, and accordions in their performances. Bands such as Planxty and The Bothy Band played songs that added a rock and roll element to Irish folk sounds.

The most popular Irish musicians have blended a more international sound with the Irish gift for storytelling. In the 1980s and 1990s, artists such as U2, Sinéad O'Connor, The Cranberries, and Enya rose to the top of the music charts. Today, Irish artists such as Hozier, Niall Horan, and The Script entertain millions of people around the world.

Some of the most celebrated actors performing in movies today come from Ireland. Saoirse Ronan has been nominated for three Academy Awards, for her roles in *Lady Bird*, *Brooklyn*, and *Atonement*. Liam Neeson has appeared in dozens of films, including *Star Wars: Episode I—The Phantom Menace* and *The Dark Knight Rises*. In 1994, he received an Academy Award nomination for his role in *Schindler's List*. Pierce Brosnan is one of only three non-British actors to play James Bond.

Saoirse Ronan won a Golden Globe Award in 2018 for her performance in *Lady Bird*.

Arts and Entertainment by the Numbers

4,391 Words in the longest sentence in James Joyce's *Ulysses*.

1726 Year *Gulliver's Travels* was published.

22 Number of Grammy Awards won by U2, the most of any rock band.

Arts and Entertainment

Ireland is well known for its long tradition and history of arts and entertainment. The misty hillsides, open spaces, and struggles with war and famine have bred a long line of poets, artists, and storytellers. These **ambassadors** have spread Irish culture and tradition throughout the world.

Dublin-born author James Joyce wrote epic works of **prose**, such as *Finnegans Wake* and *Dubliners*, that often portrayed life in Ireland. Oscar Wilde, also from Dublin, wrote *The Picture of Dorian Gray* and *The Importance of Being Earnest*. Other notable Irish writers include Bram Stoker, the author of *Dracula*, Jonathan Swift, who wrote *Gulliver's Travels*, Samuel Beckett, the writer of *Waiting for Godot*, and the celebrated poet, William Butler Yeats.

James Joyce was born in Dublin in 1882.

Gulliver's Travels was made into a movie starring Jack Black. Released in 2010, it shows Gulliver visiting a variety of different lands, including Lilliput, home to miniature-sized people.

24 Exploring Countries

The most common place for visitors to see the Irish language in practice is on road signs. Any traffic sign in Ireland with words must include Irish. Most signs have the Irish language in italics with the English in large letters underneath. However, there are some parts of Ireland that have Irish-only road signs. These areas are called Gaeltachtai.

Scattered throughout Ireland, Gaeltachtai are where large numbers of people still speak Irish as their main language. The most populous Gaeltacht is around Galway, on the country's west coast. Other major Gaeltachtai can be found in the counties of Cork, Clare, and Mayo. These areas are officially recognized and protected by the Irish government.

Ireland is also home to many other cultural groups. Polish people make up the largest minority group in Ireland. There are also small pockets of people from Romania, Lithuania, Latvia, Brazil, and the United Kingdom. Most immigrants live in or near Dublin, helping it to become one of Europe's most **cosmopolitan** and **multicultural** cities. Up to 200 languages are spoken in the city.

Cultural Groups by the Numbers

122,515 Number of Polish people living in Ireland, making up more than 2.5 percent of the population.

40% Portion of Irish people who speak Irish.

612,018 Number of people in Ireland who speak a language other than Irish or English at home.

The Polish community has established a presence in Dublin, with many immigrants starting businesses of their own.

Irish athletes excel in many other sports as well, with several playing in the top tiers of their sport. Conor McGregor is a mixed martial arts athlete from Dublin. Competing in the Ultimate Fighting Championship (UFC), he has become world-famous for his fighting skills and feisty personality. McGregor has the distinction of being the first UFC athlete to hold titles in two weight divisions at the same time. In 2015, he won the featherweight championship. He won the lightweight championship the following year.

With its rolling green terrain, Ireland is a perfect place to train golfers. Padraig Harrington is known as one of the greatest golfers to come out of Ireland. Harrington is the first golfer from the Republic of Ireland to win multiple major championships. He won the British Open two years in a row, in 2007 and 2008, along with the 2008 Professional Golfers' Association (PGA) Championship.

Roy Keane is widely considered to be Ireland's greatest soccer player. Keane played midfield for Manchester United for 12 years, and won the Champions League tournament as the team captain. He also represented Ireland at the World Cup.

Horse racing has a long history in Ireland, dating back to at least 60 AD. Today, many of the major derbies are held at the Curragh Racecourse, in County Kildare.

Sports by the Numbers

82,300 Number of spectators that fill Dublin's Croke Park stadium for the All-Ireland Finals of Gaelic football each year.

1928 Year Pat O'Callaghan won the hammer throw event at the Olympic Games in Amsterdam, giving Ireland its first Olympic gold medal.

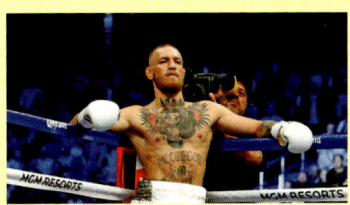

4.3 Million Number of North Americans who watched Conor McGregor box against Floyd Mayweather on pay-per-view in 2017.

Republic of Ireland

Mapping the Republic of Ireland

We use many tools to interpret maps and to understand the locations of features such as cities, states, lakes, and rivers. The map below has many tools to help interpret information on the Republic of Ireland.

Map of the Republic of Ireland

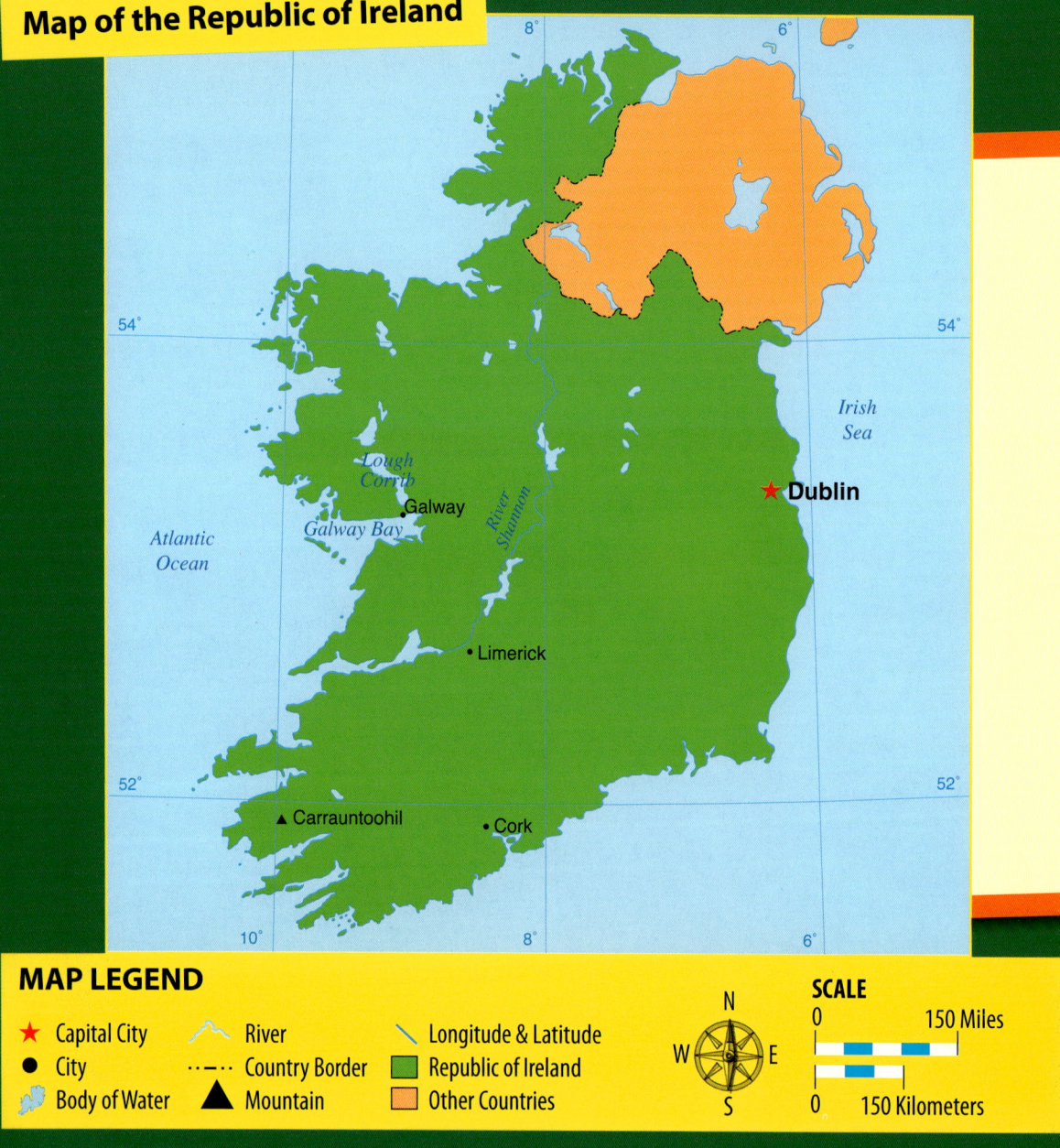

Mapping Tools

- The compass rose shows north, south, east, and west. The points in-between represent northeast, northwest, southeast, and southwest.

- The map scale shows that the distances on a map represent much longer distances in real life. If you measure the distance between objects on a map, you can use the map scale to calculate the actual distance in miles or kilometers between those two points.

- The lines of latitude and longitude are long lines that appear on maps. The lines of latitude run east to west and measure how far north or south of the equator a place is located. The lines of longitude run north to south and measure how far east or west of the Prime Meridian a place is located. A location on a map can be found by using the two numbers where latitude and longitude meet. This number is called a coordinate and is written using degrees and direction. For example, the city of Dublin would be found at 53°N and 6°W on a map.

Map It!

Using the map and the appropriate tools, complete the activities below.

Locating with latitude and longitude
1. Which lake is located at 53°N and 9°W?
2. Which mountain is located at 51°N and 10°W?
3. Which city is found at 53°N and 9°W?

Distances between points
4. Using the map scale and a ruler, calculate the approximate distance between Dublin and Galway.
5. Using the map scale and a ruler, calculate the approximate distance between Cork and Limerick.
6. Using the map scale and a ruler, calculate the approximate length of the River Shannon.

ANSWERS 1. Lough Corrib 2. Carrauntoohil 3. Galway 4. 129 miles (208 km) 5. 62 miles (99 km) 6. 161 miles (259 km)

Quiz Time

Test your knowledge of the Republic of Ireland by answering these questions.

1 How many counties make up the Republic of Ireland?

2 What is the nickname given to Ireland for its many shades of green?

3 What is the Republic of Ireland's national symbol?

4 What natural fuel is found in Irish bogs?

5 Where is the *Book of Kells* kept?

6 In what city is Silicon Docks located?

7 Which economic sector employs the most Irish workers?

8 Which Irish high king was killed by Vikings?

9 What food crop failed in the 1840s, leading to the Great Famine?

10 What two Irish sports are represented by the GAA?

ANSWERS
1. 26
2. Emerald Isle
3. Shamrock
4. Peat
5. Trinity College
6. Dublin
7. Service sector
8. Brian Boru
9. Potatoes
10. Gaelic football and hurling

30 Exploring Countries

Key Words

ambassadors: people who act as representatives for a country or activity

ancestry: referring to people in one's family or cultural group in past times

archaeologists: scientists who study human life and activities by examining objects

artifact: an object made by humans

bogs: areas of soft, wet earth

Bronze Age: a prehistoric period when bronze was the prime resource for making tools and weapons

civil war: a war between citizens of the same country

clans: groups of families that are related to each other

commodity: an economic resource or product

constitution: a written document stating a country's or area's basic principles and laws

cosmopolitan: containing people from many countries

economies: the wealth and resources of countries or areas

employment rate: the percentage of the labor force that is working

European Union (EU): a political and economic organization that has more than two dozen member countries

eurozone: the group of EU nations whose national currency is the euro

exported: sold goods to another country

famine: an extreme scarcity of food

Gulf Stream: the current of warm water that flows from the Gulf of Mexico toward Europe

imports: buys goods from other countries

Iron Age: a prehistoric period when iron was the main resource for making tools and weapons

mammals: animals that have hair or fur and drink milk from their mother

minerals: natural substances that are neither plants nor animals

multicultural: containing several cultural or ethnic groups

nomadic: moving often

parliamentary democracy: a form of government in which the party with the greatest representation in the legislature forms the government

peninsula: an area of land surrounded by water on three sides

plains: flat, treeless areas

progressive: favoring progess, change, and improvement

prose: language written in its ordinary form

renewable energy: forms of energy produced from resouces that will not be used up over time

republic: a form of government in which the head of state is elected

rural: of the country

spawn: to release or deposit eggs

species: groups of individuals with common characteristics

start-up: a new company

Stone Age: a prehistoric period when weapons and tools were made of stone or organic materials

treaty: a negotiated agreement

urban: relating to a town or city

Index

Achill Island 6
Anglo-Irish Treaty 19
Atlantic Ocean 6, 7, 8, 9, 28

Blarney Castle 12
Book of Kells 12, 30
Boru, Brian 17, 30

Carrauntoohil 6, 7, 28, 29
Celtic Sea 6, 7
Celts 16, 17, 22
Cliffs of Moher 8, 9, 13
Clontarf, Battle of 17, 18
Cork 12, 13, 23, 29

Dáil Éireann 21
Dingle Peninsula 13
Dublin 5, 7, 12, 13, 14, 15, 17, 19, 20, 23, 24, 26, 27, 28, 29, 30
Dublin Castle 12, 13

European Union (EU) 4, 6, 20
exports 15

Fenians 19
Five Fifths 17

Gaelic football 26, 27, 30
Gaelic language 22
Gaeltachtai 23
Galway 9, 13, 23, 26, 28, 29
Great Famine 18, 19, 20, 30

hurling 26, 30

imports 15
Irish Free State 19
Irish Republican Army (IRA) 19
Irish Sea 6, 7, 18, 28

Joyce, James 24, 25

MacGillycuddy's Reeks 7, 8

Northern Ireland 6, 7, 19

Oireachtas 21

peat 8, 11, 30

River Liffey 7
River Shannon 6, 7, 28, 29

Seanad Éireann 21
Silicon Docks 14, 30
St. Patrick's Day 13
St. Stephen's Green 12

Trinity College 12, 30

United Kingdom 6, 19, 23

Vikings 17, 18, 30

Wilde, Oscar 24

zinc 11

Republic of Ireland 31

Log on to www.av2books.com

AV² by Weigl brings you media enhanced books that support active learning. Go to www.av2books.com, and enter the special code found on page 2 of this book. You will gain access to enriched and enhanced content that supplements and complements this book. Content includes video, audio, weblinks, quizzes, a slideshow, and activities.

AV² Online Navigation

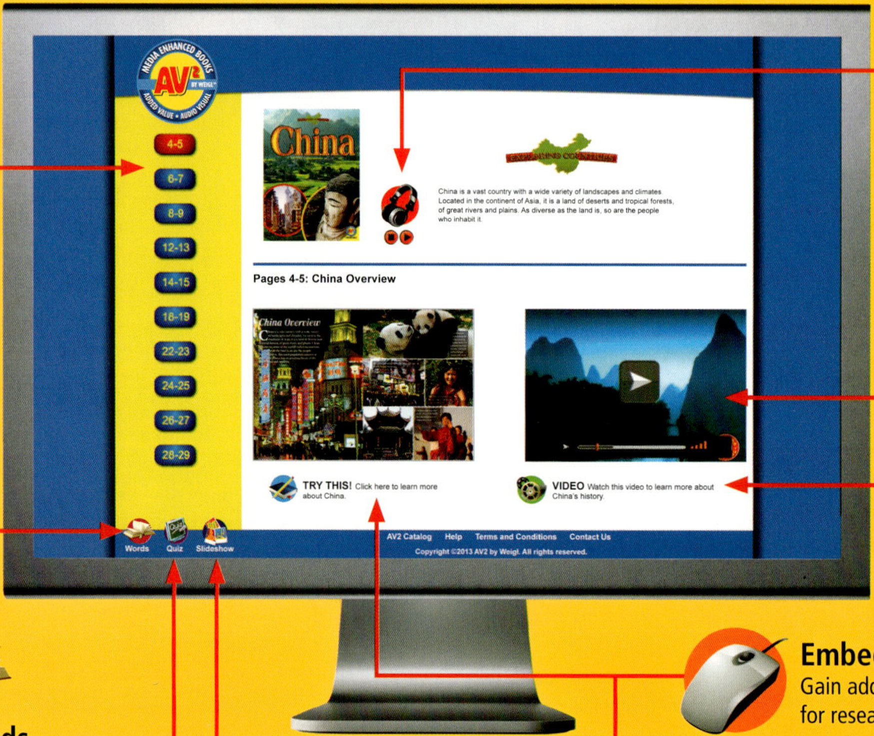

Book Pages
AV² pages directly correspond to pages in the book.

Audio
Listen to sections of the book read aloud.

Video
Watch informative video clips.

Key Words
Study vocabulary, and complete a matching word activity.

Embedded Weblinks
Gain additional information for research.

Quizzes
Test your knowledge.

Slideshow
View images and captions, and prepare a presentation.

Try This!
Complete activities and hands-on experiments.

AV² was built to bridge the gap between print and digital. We encourage you to tell us what you like and what you want to see in the future.

Sign up to be an AV² Ambassador at www.av2books.com/ambassador.

Due to the dynamic nature of the internet, some of the URLs and activities provided as part of AV² by Weigl may have changed or ceased to exist. AV² by Weigl accepts no responsibility for any such changes. All media enhanced books are regularly monitored to update addresses and sites in a timely manner. Contact AV² by Weigl at 1-866-649-3445 or av2books@weigl.com with any questions, comments, or feedback.